THE SECOND ACT

MY RECOVERY OF A RUPTURED BRAIN ANEURYSM

ANDREW DAVIE

For Susan Fago

ACKNOWLEDGMENTS

Thank you Tyler for the copyedits. Emma, Lydia, Dan, Jess, Dr. Kim, Dr. V, Dr. H, Dr. Pressley, Prof. Hida, at the Chicago School of Professional Psychology. Stephanie, Michelle, Zach, James, and the staff at Brain Injury Services. Tess, John, and The Lynn Oswald Brain Aneurysm Support Group. Jan, Bryant, and Alesia. Jay Garfield. Uncle Bruckles. Johnny K. Heather. Thelma. "Aunt" Coarole. Adam, Laura, Owen, Simon, Mom and Dad.

CONTENTS

THE FANTASTIC NOTE WHEN THE RABBIT BITES ITS OWN HEAD OFF

The above title is a quotation from Dr. Gonzo in the book *Fear and Loathing in Las Vegas* written by Hunter S. Thompson. Gonzo says the line while he is in a bathtub submerged up to his eyes in opaque green water; the result of putting in too many Japanese bath salts. The good doctor has also taken enough acid to satisfy all of Haight/Ashbury and is hallucinating.

He requests Thompson throw a portable radio into the bathtub and electrocute Gonzo while the song "White Rabbit" by Jefferson Airplane plays at that specific part of the song mentioned in the title. Although Gonzo might very well achieve enlightenment, or have some other epiphany of higher understanding, he would also be killed. Instead, Thompson throws a grapefruit into the tub.

Later, when accosted by an angry Dr. Gonzo, who is displeased at his wish not being granted, Thompson threatens to mace Gonzo until he calms down. Though you might have difficulty seeing any corollaries here to ruptured brain aneurysm recovery, I'm going to do my darndest to establish one.

Early on in my healing from a ruptured brain aneurysm, sometime during the first year, my abstract thinking was virtually non-existent. It suddenly returned one evening while I was completing a worksheet in which the goal was to infer information about dogs, types of dog collars, and their respective owners. It was as if someone had cast a spell on me. Naively, I expected the rest of the recovery to be similar. Like Dr. Gonzo in the bathtub, I had assumed the bulk of my healing would happen just as quickly and suddenly, like being struck by lightning, or in his case, riding the lightning.

In no time, I would begin to feel like my old self again. The same goals I'd had before the aneurysm: starting a family and becoming a successful author would mean as much as they had before and would essentially provide me with a drive and motivation to get out of bed each day.

Of course, this did not happen. I no longer had the same desire to start a family, and publishing a book did not alter the landscape as I had assumed. It took a while, about three years, for me to adjust to feeling more comfortable.

At the end of the previous addendum, "Playing With House Money", I mentioned a quotation by Albert Camus which suggested that even though I knew the recovery would still be difficult, I was motivated and driven. That remains the same. Although, I want to re-enforce the idea that the journey won't suddenly have become easier by Years 4 and 5, but I certainly feel more capable and confident these days.

In March 2020, almost two years after the aneurysm, I had gotten a job at a tutoring center near where I lived. I figured since I had been a teacher, why not return to the profession—especially since I could still work. I had also just begun dating again. I was on track to resume my life after a few speed bumps. Of course, by April the following month, the job was canceled due to the onset of a worldwide pandemic in the form of COVID-19.

As a result, I would move back in with my parents for a little over a year. My mother drove to my house, picked me up, and brought me back with her. Initially, I assumed I would stay with them for a few weeks. Once I realized I had nothing to return to, a few weeks became indefinite. While not desirable by any stretch, this chain of events turned out to have a silver lining. Rather than try to build something that resembled my old life, but wasn't going to provide solace, I would be able to focus exclusively on adjusting and a future that would be fulfilling. I began to ask myself if my former goals weren't going to motivate me on a bad day, what could I do?

This is also where Simone De Beauvoir's *Ethics of Ambiguity* comes into play. I had been listening to a philosophy podcast titled *Philosophize This!* And an episode about Simone De Beauvoir resonated with me. She posits that we are both subjects and objects in the world. The tension we feel ultimately comes from the tug-of-war between those two states. We do not like being unable to define ourselves by one description, but the reality is we are both. According to De Beauvoir, we need to "will our own freedom" but since everything is interrelated, we also need to "will the freedom of others."

Rather than focus exclusively on something that would only make me feel fulfilled, I realized I also needed to incorporate the wellbeing of others. When I thought back to the few times I'd felt at ease over the last few years, it always had to do with the reassurance from another survivor, usually in a support group or responding on a message board, that what I had been experiencing during my recovery was not unique.

Instead of returning to the teaching profession, I decided I would change careers. Technically, this would be the fifth different career after recruiter, office manager, sell-side broker/options trader, and teacher. Although I have made some money from writing, I wouldn't count it as a career. I realized if I became a therapist, I could provide support for other people who needed guidance, which would also make me feel fulfilled as well. I did some research, found that clinical mental health counseling would be suitable, and applied to schools. I was accepted to The Chicago School of Professional Psychology's Washington D.C. Campus, and I began taking classes in January 2022.

A RECAP OF 2020-2021

The year I lived with my parents during the height of COVID, it was deciding to change careers, receiving Somatic Experience Therapy, and time, that ultimately helped me adjust. That's not to say I wouldn't have difficult days in the future, but those three changes were what allowed me to move forward with more confidence.

Previously, I was overwhelmed with no direction, and I had trouble imagining what sort of value my life would have since none of my previous goals seemed to matter. I had focused almost all my attention on writing with the hope that getting published would somehow provide meaning.

Rick Rubin's podcast interview with Andre Benjamin does a phenomenal job articulating how finally achieving an artistic goal like publishing a book, making a film, or recording an album, does not magically "fill the hole, most creative types are plagued by." My first book, *Pavement*, was released in 2019, so it was after the aneurysm and it felt like a double whammy. Not only would I have to adjust to life post-aneurysm, but the very thing that had been providing drive for me (publishing a book) didn't solve my dilemma when it finally happened.

Teaching, while enjoyable, had always felt like a means to an end. Plus, my experience substitute teaching at my previous school the year after my aneurysm, hadn't been fulfilling. Eventually, I was able to teach an online creative writing class as an after-school elective, but I discovered my desire wasn't there anymore.

Lastly, I had always assumed I would get married and start a family. After some reflection, I realized most of that desire had been conditioned by societal expectations. Although I did enjoy being in a relationship with someone, much of the trajectory of how I had wanted things to play out were due to the fact I assumed that having a family was what a good life included.

In the film *Thief*, James Caan plays an ex-convict who, while in prison, made a collage of all the things he would want in his life when he was released. The collage included most societal expectations such as getting married, having children, the house in the suburbs, car, etc. During my downtime with my parents, I realized that while I hadn't made a collage, I was in essence doing a similar thing.

I had also touched on this previously, but the way I processed emotions had changed. Not only that, but rather than accept things would be different for the foreseeable future, I only focused on whether it would return. In 2019, while visiting a friend in New Hampshire, sitting on a dock at the lake during sunset, rather than enjoying what I could connect with, I spent most of my time focusing on how the serenity and beauty of nature had little emotional effect. Intellectuality, I knew how wonderful it all was, and I kept expecting an emotional exhilaration.

What was particularly interesting was that during the first year of my recovery, I would frequently get emotionally overwhelmed and cry. Then, suddenly, at one point the opposite happened. I became somewhat emotionally detached.

The final date I went on before COVID contributed to my decision to step away from dating; I went out to lunch with a very attractive and funny person. I remember thinking to myself that I should be sexually aroused and want to see her again. The analogy I made previously was that it was emotionally and physiologically similar to watching a documentary film about paint drying.

All of these differences necessitated a major change.

RELEVANT MOVIE QUOTATIONS

"I told you not to stop. Now let's go."

The above quotation is from a scene in *Apocalypse Now!* Captain Willard has already accepted a mission to terminate Colonel's Kurtz's command, and he travels to the colonel's compound on a PBR boat. At one point, the boat's crew open fire on a group of locals. It's a massacre, but at least one person survives. The chief of the boat says they need to take a wounded woman to get help, which may possibly put the mission in jeopardy as a result. Captain Willard casually removes his firearm, shoots the wounded woman, kills her, and says the line matter-of-factly, with no discernable inflection in his tone. I felt like this was a perfect metaphor for my lack of emotional connection.

"What is this salty discharge?"

Jerry Seinfeld says this during a scene in which he cries for what seems to be the first time. In a different scene, he's visited by the father of a fan of his. The fan is a boy who has a severe immune deficiency and must live sequestered behind plastic. As the father tells the story of his son, he begins to cry. Elaine, who's also at the table, begins to cry and hands the father and Jerry some napkins. The father and Elaine blot their eyes while Jerry uses the napkin to wipe his mouth. This comes to mind frequently when I'm unable to experience the weight or gravity of an emotion. My body will prepare itself to cry and I'll get right up to the precipice where I can feel the tears beginning to form, but they never arrive. I have begun to wonder what happens to those emotions: is it like a dream deferred? And, boom, an unexpected Langston Hughes reference buried within a Seinfeld reference. I dare you to find another book about ruptured brain aneurysm recovery which can juxtapose those two references.

"Mongo only pawn in game of life."

Former college and professional football player Alex Karras says this as the character Mongo in the film *Blazing Saddles*. It is one of the more poignant things said in the movie, which is one of the greatest comedies of all time. There had been times when I would think about this line, especially when I felt the need to have figured more things out with not only the recovery but the direction of my life.

"Now look, I'm not a cop, I don't know how he did it, all I know is that he DID it."

Sam Bowden (Nick Nolte) says this in the movie *Cape Fear* when he's telling a police officer that Max Cady (Robert De Niro), an ex-convict, was responsible for the death of the Bowden family's dog. Originally, the police officer asks if the Bowdens let their dog out, and Sam says they didn't. The police officer infers that Cady could be charged with breaking and entering, and Sam says Cady didn't break into their house. At that point, Sam says the above line. Sometimes, this is what I would think of when I would try to articulate the type of the different changes I've experienced. Trying to accurately describe my balance difficulties and the emotional processing differences are difficult to do. Stepping off a merry-go-round is a great analogy for what my vision problems are like, but I have yet to find another good one.

"No matter what he's tried, and he's tried everything."

This is from the opening narration of a film titled *The Beaver*, which according to *Wikipedia* is "about

Walter Black, a depressed executive, who hits rock-bottom when his wife kicks him out of the house. At his lowest point, he begins to use a beaver hand puppet to communicate with people and overcome his issues." Before he discovers said puppet, he attempts a whole slew of self-help solutions and none of them are effective. At one point, earlier in my recovery, I revisited different forms of physical therapy and acupuncture, hoping it could somehow "reset" my vestibular processing. I also looked for existential answers by reading the *I Ching*; while these endeavors might very well be helpful, they did not provide the results I had sought.

"Dreams, expectations ... never happened man, and the worst, the worst; nothing happens."

This line is said by the character Stiles in the film *The Jericho Mile*. Previously, Stiles had made a deal with other prisoners to arrange a conjugal visit with his wife. They double-cross him and use the opportunity to smuggle drugs into the prison. Stiles gives up the ruse and, as a result, the drugs get seized. While upset at the fact he's been double-crossed, Stiles also realizes he needs to go into isolation to be protected and he won't be able to see his wife, who has also just given birth to their daughter. The very thing that's been giving him hope has now been taken away.

I'm reminded of the *Stockdale Paradox*, in which author Jim Collins had been interviewing former Admiral James Stockdale about his prisoner-of-war experience in Vietnam. Stockdale suggested his survival was attributed to the following: "You must never confuse faith that you will prevail in the end—which you can never afford to lose—with the discipline to confront the most brutal facts of your current reality, whatever they might be." I think this is applicable to recovery, life, and more. Being able to manage expectations is crucial.

BACK TO SCHOOL

Most of the lyrics of the song "School" by Nirvana discuss the singer's lament about how there was no recess that day. As I got ready to return to life as a student, I had to manage my expectations. This would be my second experience in graduate school. I got my MFA in my early thirties, and I began to wonder whether this was the beginning of a pattern. Every 10 years, would I return to higher education? Going into the counseling program, I had certain assumptions of what the profession would entail, what classes would be like, etcetera. I also kept thinking about the song "School" and, more importantly, Jason Everman. The song "School" appears on the album *Bleach* which was released by Nirvana in 1989, two years before they would change music with the release of *Nevermind.* Jason Everman is credited on the album, although he doesn't play. He paid for the recording fee.

Everman provides an interesting and motivating story in that he was technically a member of Nirvana, and subsequently joined Soundgarden. At one point, he read the autobiography of Renaissance artist Benvenuto Cellini, who suggested a well-rounded person is an artist, warrior, and philosopher. Everman left the band in which he currently played, Mind Funk, and enlisted in the US Army, eventually serving with the Rangers, and after with the Special Forces. His dedication was motivating, and while I wasn't going to be joining the armed forces, I still thought of his transition.

Going back to school again was interesting, especially as someone who only had a humanities background. Diagnosing was my first in-person class and it was overwhelming, but the professor checked in with me during a break and assured me I would adjust. She was correct. One of my next classes was theories, which was a little closer to being in my wheelhouse, and the professor was also helpful. Not to mention, one of the first theories we read about was existential theory, which dealt with a lot of the themes I'd been reading about and experiencing firsthand during the previous few years.

As I continued to take classes, I was fortunate to

have some very caring and considerate professors who have allowed me to feel comfortable in this endeavor. Similarly, I have made some good friends, which has all helped me to adjust. Below, I've included three papers I wrote for my Diversity and Multiculturalism, Theories, and Methods of Research classes that do a pretty good job continuing to incorporate elements of my recovery while providing insight to what the experience at school has been like.

EXCERPTS OF A CULTURAL IDENTITY ANALYSIS PAPER

One of the first jobs I had after graduating from college was working as the office manager for a non-equity, bus-and-truck, touring theater company. Our office was located in Times Square. I worked at the company from the beginning of 2001 until 2005. One element that made the experience unique was that I would walk through Times Square and frequently come into contact with people from every imaginable background. Since I had grown up in New York City, I was already familiar with many cultural differences. Eventually, I switched job paths and worked in finance, which was a completely different environment. The main pursuit continued to be writing.

While in graduate school for creative writing, I decided to become a teacher and applied for a Fulbright Grant to teach English in Macau. Living in Macau and subsequently Hong Kong for two years helped to shape my worldview. Since I had grown up in New York City, I had been immersed in a variety of different cultures, but it had been a proverbial melting pot in which everyone was essentially a New Yorker, even if they had retained most of their cultural heritage. However, living in Southeast Asia meant a complete change of customs and practices. This provided more concrete examples to help shape my worldview

In 2017, I started taking Prozac to address symptoms of obsessive-compulsive disorder (OCD) that was predicated on an irrational fear that I would contract HIV from everyday encounters. The symptoms started in 2008 and I tried analytical therapy with mixed results. Though medication had been suggested, I was hesitant about potential side effects. However, even though concepts like personal space don't exist in Southeast Asia, I was able to acclimate pretty well. During the two years I lived there, I only had one extreme case that caused me to spiral out of control.

I had gotten a haircut from a barber who shaved my neck with a straight razor. I stayed after my turn ended since a friend of mine was also getting his hair cut. He happened to visit the same barber who shaved my friend's neck with the same straight razor he'd used for me but without changing or sterilizing the blade. As a result, I had a breakdown in which I needed to call my brother, who was attending medical school in the United States, to help talk me off the proverbial ledge.

In 2014, when I moved to Virginia, the situation got dire. What had been somewhat manageable became virtually unbearable—to the point where I would ask students to open and close doors so I wouldn't have to touch the doorknob. As a result, I finally decided to start taking Prozac. Fortunately, the medication worked, and my symptoms would only reveal themselves in extreme cases of anxiety but were easily vanquished. These days, I'm no longer worried about getting AIDS from touching doorknobs as I had been during the worst of the experience. However, when my anxiety flares up, I still construct scenarios that include more logical though uncommon outcomes, such as accidentally getting stuck with a hypodermic needle. However, I'm still taking Prozac, I'm aware of the response I may have if my OCD is triggered, and I am taking steps to address it.

On June 29, 2018, I had a ruptured brain aneurysm. According to The Bee Foundation (2022), 1 in 50 people in the US have a brain aneurysm, and 4 out of 10 with a rupture will die. Each year, 500,000 deaths worldwide occur from brain aneurysms and half the victims are younger than fifty. At the time, I had just turned forty. My first book was going to be published the following year, I had not renewed my teaching contract, and I was applying to Ph.D. programs for creative writing. On the morning of June 29th, I was going to fly to visit my parents. I collapsed on the jetway before I could board the plane, which ended up saving my life.

Upon reflection, I realize I processed my physical and emotional recoveries separately. At first, I needed a cane and a guard belt to walk, had double vision, and had poor balance. By the end of the first year, I was able to walk without a cane and could participate in limited physical exercise. I had also assumed the rest of the recovery would happen just as quickly. At some point, I imagined I would begin to feel similar to the way I had felt before the aneurysm. I remember distinctly thinking I would begin to feel like my old self again, similar to putting on an old jacket that still fit. However, I was to learn that while certain elements of my life would remain, many of my previous goals and desires would change.

I also had to recognize the way I processed emotions were different. It took about three years of therapy and hard work to acclimate to life after the aneurysm. For example, before the injury, I had imagined my life would be complete if I started a family of my own. Growing up, I had been conditioned to believe the nuclear family was the ideal. The goal in life would be to acquire a house, car, dog, and 2.5 children. Eventually, I was fortunate enough to realize I didn't need anything I didn't already have to feel fulfilled.

I meet the criteria to be considered disabled since I still have some minor physical limitations, such as vision and balance issues. However, I don't think of myself as disabled. I don't know if I have ever been discriminated against due to my situation since it has never been overt or direct.

I had originally thought to return to teaching and got a job as a tutor that was to start in April 2020. However, the job was canceled due to COVID and I moved in with my parents for a little over a year. Again, this was an opportunity that didn't exist for many people, and I was both aware and grateful I could live with them. During the year I lived with my family, I reassessed my life and realized providing support for people in recovery would be a more fulfilling endeavor than teaching. Therefore, I applied to and began a Clinical Mental Health Counseling program at The Chicago School of Professional Psychology in Washington D.C.

As a result of my upbringing, lived experience, and outlook, I tend to easily accept most worldviews different from my own, whether they pertain to race, ethnicity, religion, or sexual orientation. My experience has continued to help provide perspective and be more aware of the discrimination some people endure based on less visible afflictions. Since having the aneurysm and beginning the counseling program, I have become much more aware of how difficult it is for people to be transparent about who they are and feel comfortable doing so.

As a result of all these experiences, I have a more nuanced understanding of what Henry David Thoreau meant when he suggested most people lead lives of quiet desperation (Thoreau, 1854). While my view hasn't necessarily changed, I've decided to play a more active role in society. I would have been comfortable with people being able to do their own thing and living their own lives, but I've also recognized that I must address perceived wrongs. A line I often think of from the movie *The Confession*: "It's hard to know the right thing to do, but once you know, it's hard not to do it" (Jones, 1999).

I believe my viewpoint has been shaped by some of my experiences best put forth in the Ecological model by Urie Bronfenbrenner. Beginning with my immediate interactions with my family, and moving outward, my personality, understanding, and everything, has been shaped by these experiences.

I have been fortunate to have found most, if not all, my life experiences pleasant and fulfilling. I have had opportunities to explore the world, and due to these various factors, I have developed an inclusive and empathetic view. When I had reached a point in my recovery where I could begin considering the future, I decided to become a Clinical Mental Health Counselor.

The change of career path was due to my desire to help other people who struggled with their recovery from a brain injury. As a result, I also became much more involved in advocacy and helping people who might not have the resources to help themselves. I had always recognized I was in a privileged position where I could be an ally, but my injury was what spurred me to be more involved. As a result, I believe I'll be able to provide support to clients who are struggling with their recoveries, and I'll be able to use my privileged position to call attention to an unjust situation or try to create change when it is needed. I won't be able to understand what anyone experiences as a result of bigotry, but as someone who's made a significant adjustment during recovery, I do understand how these traumas can be overwhelming.

The important thing, moving forward as a counselor, is that I will be aware of these situations and be able to provide support. People will have preconceived ideas about me based on my appearance and our initial conversation. I don't have any control over that. However, I explained that since I've experienced some traumatic events in my life, I will be able to reveal a vulnerability that will hopefully allow for a strong therapeutic alliance.

To summarize, moving forward, I will never be able to understand anyone else's lived experience. I have been fortunate to have a privileged life in every capacity due to some circumstances within my control, but most were decided for me. Since I have managed OCD, and continue to recover from a ruptured brain aneurysm, I have a better understanding of the depth and magnitude of some traumatic experiences and hopefully, that will be conducive to developing an empathetic relationship. Most importantly, while I had been content with a more passive role in life, I have realized I need to be more active both politically and culturally. Unfortunately, too many people are disenfranchised today and can't affect change. However, I am in that position. I have recognized the right thing, and I look forward to doing it.

References

About brain aneurysms. The Bee Foundation. (2022, January 29). Retrieved October 27, 2022, from https://www.thebeefoundation.org/brain-aneurysm/.

El Dorado Pictures. (1999). *The Confession. IMDb*. USA. Retrieved November 19, 2022, from https://www.imdb.com/title/tt0128137/.
Thoreau, H. D. (1854). *Walden. Project Gutenberg*. Retrieved November 19, 2022, from https://www.gutenberg.org/files/205/205-h/205-h.htm.

REFLECTION PAPER ON EXISTENTIAL THERAPY

According to Corey (2017), the existentialist tradition tries to balance the incongruity of the finite limits of human existence with unlimited potential and opportunities. People want to be able to give themselves an accurate label or have a specific self-identity, but since everything is always changing, it remains difficult to do that. Ultimately, people have anxiety due to various factors associated with trying to balance this ambiguity, including the freedom to make their own choices, a need for meaning, and possessing self-awareness.

Corey (2017) suggests the existential therapist can help clients recognize that learning how to tolerate ambiguity and how to live without props can be a necessary phase in the journey from dependence to autonomy. Essentially, the counselor can work with the patient to feel more comfortable with defining their identity, searching for meaning in their life, and having positive relationships with others.

On June 29th, 2018, I had a ruptured brain aneurysm and subarachnoid hemorrhage. While I was able to recover well physically, the emotional recovery took the longest time, and I wrestled with many existential concepts such as what is the meaning of my life now? Unfortunately, many of the goals I had had, which I felt added value to my life, suddenly didn't seem as important—or, due to my difficulty in making emotional connections, seemed unattainable. For a few years, I tried to force the issue and continued to use my previous goals to motivate me but after a while, I realized it was a moot point.

At one point, I had wanted to have a serious relationship with someone and possibly start a family. In the addendum to my memoir *Land of Allusions*, titled "Playing with House Money" (2022), I wrote the following:

> Uncertainty with what the future holds for me is sometimes overwhelming. The goals I'd had before the aneurysm now seem either unattainable or no longer worthwhile. It is difficult to be consistently motivated. For example, I had always assumed I would get married or start a family. But

the recovery has forced me to reexamine this since I have difficulty making emotional connections now. I may or may not be able to have a relationship with someone, and part of the reason it had been difficult to adjust is that there had seemed to be little else to make life worth living. Most of the time, I would measure everything against a quotation from the film *Into the Wild*: "Happiness is only real when shared." At some point, I thought, before the aneurysm, I would meet the right person and be able to truly fulfill the tenet of that quotation.

I had to reassess my goals and become comfortable with the uncertainty of not necessarily knowing what direction my life would take. Having the chance to continue to recover without distractions was instrumental in me feeling less anxious. I also read *Man's Search for Meaning* by Viktor Frankl, in which I read that people could find meaning and fulfillment during even the most difficult of circumstances. Reading about Frankl's experience as a prisoner in multiple concentrations camps gave me the terminology to articulate what I had been feeling. Over time, I was able to feel less overwhelmed about my situation.

Due to my experience, the values discussed in existential therapy mirror what I think is important and since those principles helped me to adjust during my recovery, I believe existential therapy is valid.

However, while I was able to make use of existential therapeutic practice to adjust to life after a trauma, it isn't necessarily a universal practice that would be good for everyone. People who would benefit most from existential therapy are those, like myself, who are recovering from trauma or who are having difficulty figuring out their identity or their purpose. People who don't believe that there is a universal objective meaning to life would benefit from the existential approach. As a result, existential therapy would work well for people of different cultures, genders, and affectional identities, since anyone can use the theory to address any difficulty they might be experiencing.

Existential therapy would probably not benefit people who are from a marginalized group, where it would be difficult for them to solve issues by themselves. Since existential therapy requires the client to make their own decisions, it might not be easy for people who face an unfair systematic disadvantage. People who can't affect change or make choices by themselves would probably have a difficult time with this particular type of therapy. Similarly, it might not be the easiest practice for someone who is devoutly religious and believes in a higher objective truth. Existential therapy relies on a subjective interpretation by the client of what is important and valuable, and that perspective might clash with established institutional guidelines.

Existential therapy also addresses grand large-scale dilemmas like what is the meaning of life, whereas many people would benefit from therapy that addresses problems that are smaller in scope. Plus, it takes time to address and think about these conundrums. I did not truly feel comfortable with addressing my future until after I had recovered for almost three years. Even

then, I did not have the same obligations most people face when they are approaching middle age. I am fortunate in that I had the time to exclusively address these existential issues.

References

Corey, G. (2017). *Theory and Practice of Counseling and Psychotherapy*. (10th ed.). Cengage Learning.

Davie, A. (2022). *Playing With House Money**. Self-published.

* One of the more interesting events that happened during my time in school was I emailed Irvin Yalom, one of the innovators of existential therapy who is now in his 90s, and I sent him copies of my memoir

and addendum and told him I would most likely include existential therapy into the framework of my future practice. He responded that it might take him a while to read them, but he provided his address for me to send him the books.

POST-MODERN APPROACH:
SOCIAL CONSTRUCTIONIST
THEORY AND NARRATIVE
THERAPY

According to Corey (2017), dysfunction stems from problems that are products of the cultural world or of the power relations in which the world is located. Clients are often stuck in a pattern of living a problem-saturated story that does not work and, as a result, has limited perspective (p. 386). Counselors help clients to create an alternative version of what they imagine the story to be regarding the presenting problem. The goal will be to enlarge clients' perspectives and establish new options to address their concerns.

By 2008, I had been working from home for about a year, day-trading options. Around this time, I began to develop symptoms of what would later be confirmed to be obsessive-compulsive disorder (OCD). While I experience a few universal compulsions, like repeatedly checking locks and making sure the pilot light on the stove hadn't been extinguished, the major fear was that, *somehow*, I would acquire HIV from everyday activity. Even though I had learned the only way to catch the virus would be from direct sexual contact, intravenous injection, or blood transfusion, my thought process ceased being logical. Anytime I stepped on something on the sidewalk, I thought it was a used hypodermic needle. If I touched a surface that had any condensation, I assumed it to be blood or something that could transmit the virus.

Over the next few years, I would struggle to find balance. Through therapy, I was able to adjust and in 2012, I would move to Asia to teach where I would remain for two years. Except for one difficult circumstance, I was able to remain virtually symptom-free.

I returned to the United States in 2014 and within a few years, the symptoms had returned. It got to the point where I could no longer address it on my own, so I went back to therapy. This time, I also saw a psychiatrist and was prescribed Prozac. However, before I could adjust to the medication, which thankfully worked and prevented me from experiencing symptoms, I met with a therapist concurrently. During one of our first conversations, I recall him asking me to personify the anxiety. I don't remember all of the details, but I remember him suggesting that I think of it like a bee. While he and I never spoke about this particular intervention, in retrospect it would appear to be a form of narrative therapy in which he was advising me to change my perspective. We continued to meet for several months, though eventually the Prozac took hold. Once the symptoms stopped bothering me, we tapered off our sessions (Davie, 2021).

I don't think the intervention alone would have worked for this particular affliction; I needed medication, but I find the technique to be effective. As someone who enjoys and respects the power of storytelling, I think reframing the narrative is an important part of the recovery process. More recently, I've begun seeing a Somatic Experience Therapist to help develop my ability to make emotional connections, which had been compromised by my ruptured brain aneurysm. As a result, I've also realized how much of my perspective has been shaped by societal and cultural values as opposed to my subjective personal values.

I haven't necessarily utilized specific interventions from narrative therapy, but I've been able to reframe some of my thinking and shift my perspective, which has helped make many of the experiences less overwhelming. I plan to use this technique when I begin counseling.

The social constructionist theory seems to work well for all clients, regardless of their culture, gender, religion, effectual identity, etc. Rather than conform to societal expectations, clients are encouraged to reframe their thinking and determine their values. Narrative therapy is grounded in a socio-cultural context, which makes this approach especially relevant for counseling culturally diverse clients (Corey, 2017, p. 391).

However, this same strength is also a shortcoming in that the client becomes the driving force in the session. This arrangement would not work well for clients who need the counselor to be "the expert". Though this type of therapy would work well for culturally diverse groups, it would not be the best choice for clients who need direction. As someone who has dealt with a variety of setbacks and feels comfortable with my values, regardless of how they are viewed by society, this type of therapy would work well for someone like myself.

References

Corey, G. (2017). *Theory and Practice of Counseling and Psychotherapy*. (10th ed.). Cengage Learning.

Davie, A. (2021). *Land of Allusions*. Self-published.

EXAMINING THE EFFECTS OF MUSIC, PSYCHOLOGICAL WARFARE, AND TRAUMA THROUGH NARRATIVE INQUIRY

Abstract

The purpose of this research is to be able to understand the lived experience of someone who was subjected to psychological warfare and potential trauma through the use of music. "Jorge Mitzky" was going to be arrested. He had sought papal sanctuary in a church, and law enforcement played the same songs repeatedly at deafening levels, along with other ambient noise, to persuade Mr. Mitzky to surrender of his own accord. The goal is to better comprehend the effect of these conditions on the human psyche through narrative inquiry for transferable counseling applications.

According to Confucius, "Music produces a kind of pleasure which human nature cannot do without." (Pelić, 2022). Music is inextricably linked to every aspect of our lives. However, music is also capable of providing the opposite experience. In the late 1980s, "Jorge Mitzky" was subjected to psychological warfare through the use of music. He sought safety in a church. Rather than storming the building, law enforcement attempted to coerce Mr. Mitzky to leave the church of his own free will. Law enforcement's desired objective was to inflict pain by playing songs repeatedly at decibel levels that would cause severe discomfort. For two days and nights,

they blared rock music from huge speakers directly at the nunciature at deafening levels (Buckley, 1992).

The song selection was based on a certain aesthetic, as well as the knowledge that Mitzky was a fan of opera. Similarly, Jethro Tull was added to the rotation since the band was a favorite of one of the operations leaders. For two days and nights, law enforcement was rumored to have played: "Voodoo Chile (Slight Return)" by Jimi Hendrix, "Nowhere to Run" by Martha Reeves & The Vandellas, "You're No Good" by Linda Ronstadt, "I Fought the Law" by The Clash, "You Shook Me All Night Long" by AC/DC, "Welcome to the Jungle" by Guns N' Roses, and "Too Old to Rock and Roll" by Jethro Tull (Buckley, 1992).

While all these songs could be categorized as rock music, there are some subtle and distinct differences. "Voodoo Chile" is classic rock whereas "Nowhere to Run" could be labeled as pop or soul. While Mitzky's particular situation and circumstances might be rare, it is important to understand the nuances and details of the lived experience since many clients will suffer from traumatic events. Having a better idea of that situation will help provide suitable treatment.

For my proposed research study, I would conduct a narrative inquiry into the experience Mr. Mitzky had while being subjected to music against his will. Although there have been examples of music being used during interrogation methods at places like Guantanamo Bay, I'm not so interested in the collective response of prisoners who are under capture and duress. While Mr. Mitzky was in hiding, he could still move freely within the compound. To achieve triangulation for this study, I will interview Mr. Mitzky, members of law enforcement who initiated and oversaw the operation, and members of the clergy who were in the nunciature with Mr. Mitzky. As a fan of music and knowledgeable about most of the songs that were used during this procedure, I would consider myself to be heavily embedded in the topic and able to accurately represent both an objective view, as well as capture the themes and subtleties of Mr. Mitzky's story. I plan to speak with Mr.

Mitzky multiple times over a few months so he might be able to be better prepared or might recall certain information at a later date.

Though there will be a lot of transcribing required, I will assemble a team of willing participants. Another element to be cognizant of is "The Hawthorne Effect" in which Mr. Mitzky might change some of his answers since he will know he's being studied, and therefore he might either knowingly or unknowingly provide inaccurate information. Ultimately, at the heart of this study, I'm interested in the effect the music—specifically, the song choices—had on Mr. Mitzky, and what his experience was like. Though certain historical events were transpiring at the time, I'm not interested in Mr. Mitzky's role outside of his participation in this particular event.

Before beginning our discussion, I would make sure Mr. Mitzky understood and signed off on process consent which explained his rights throughout his involvement with the study. Once that had been established, I would make sure he understood the goal of the research. Initially, I would attempt to establish a rapport with Mr. Mitzky, and ask him questions about the type of music to which he did enjoy listening. I am not a fan of opera, so I would look at this as an opportunity to learn from him. I would also disclose that when I pledged to a fraternity in college, at one point I had to repeatedly listen to the song "Like a Prayer" by Madonna for a few days. We were instructed to keep count but we ended up listening to the song so many times, I *lost* count. To this day, I can still recall most of the lyrics. Listening to that song on repeat had the desired effect of making us frustrated but those of us who were involved also developed a strange bond with the song. In fact, over the next twenty years, as one of us would get married, we would request the DJ play "Like a Prayer".

Once Mr. Mitzky and I had exchanged some pleasantries, I would confirm the songs that were used by law enforcement during the siege. First, I would want to know the effect of each genre. As an outside observer, it would appear the most "effective" songs would be heavy metal or one of the various sub-genres. For example, Jethro Tull, being more of a classic progressive rock led by a flutist, would seem counterintuitive to include on the playlist.

At this point, I would stop the interview and attempt to further establish a bond by telling him about how my nephew and I would watch Jethro Tull videos together, since my nephew is a fan of the flute. Since he's also four, my nephew thinks the lead singer/flutist Ian Anderson's name is Jethro Tull. One of their live performance videos that we watch has become a call-and-response-type situation similar to audience participation during screenings of the film *The Rocky Horror Picture Show*. When Anderson leaves the stage at one point, my nephew and I emphatically implore him to return by saying, "Come back, Jethro Tull."

Hopefully, this would be enough to establish an alliance with Mr. Mitzky, but before returning to the line of questioning, I would provide him with more trivia about Jethro Tull. The inaugural Grammy Award for Best Hard Rock/Metal Performance Vocal or Instrumental was created in 1989. It was the first year the Grammy Awards recognized this category, and Metallica and their album "...And Justice for All" was predicted to win. In one of the biggest upsets of all time, Jethro Tull won the award for their album "Crest of a Knave". After revealing this trivia, I would play the song "One" by Metallica, which includes one of the heaviest breakdowns of distorted guitars and double kick drums of all time. I would ask Mr. Mitzky about the choice of ironic songs versus abrasive-sounding ones. Though I knew the inclusion of Jethro Tull was due to a personal preference, I would want to know about its effectiveness in producing law enforcement's desired effect.

Before the study began, I consulted with Midwest postal clerk and amateur doom metal musicologist, "Louise Fury." Ms. Fury and I are both members of Generation X (born sometime between 1965-1980). She suggested going with the song "Spiritual Sacrifice" by The Hyle from Denmark played very loud. Though she loves it, she could easily see it driving someone crazy who doesn't like doom metal. Doom metal typically has a slow-paced distorted guitar sound, which would provide for a disconcerting atmosphere. I also spoke with "Apollonia Camus," a member of Generation Z (born sometime between 1997-2012) who suggested the song "False Alarm" by The Weeknd which could be classified as dance-punk or electro-rock. That was her suggestion once given the parameters. It has more of a dance beat and an upbeat tempo. These songs or drastically different from each other. Though I am interested in every aspect of what Mr. Mitzky tells me about his experience, the genre of music used is one of the main themes of interest. Therefore, I would have to be specifically aware of these questions and not allow for experimenter bias of any kind to influence Mr. Mitzky as he told his story.

Once we had gone through a few more questions about song composition and genre of music, I would ask about lyrical content. Some of the purported songs seem obvious based on their titles. I would ask Mr. Mitzky if he ever thought about the subject or metaphorical quality. Songs like "Nowhere to Run" and "You're No Good" seem obvious, as well as "Welcome to the Jungle". "I Fought the Law" is another song with clear implications in the lyrical content. I Fought the Law addresses a criminal reflecting on how he indeed fought the law and the law won. However, again this is when I would reveal the lyrics to the song "One" and ask him if he thought law enforcement possibly made a similar error that the Grammy organization made. The lyrics contain a ton of metaphors to imprisonment. Unless lyrical interpretation didn't factor into it, "One" would seem like a great choice to establish a sense of dread and foreboding. At this point, I would digress with more trivia and mention how Metallica wrote the song "One" based on the book and film adaptation *Johnny Got His Gun* about a World War One veteran who loses his arms, legs, sight, and hearing. The music video includes excerpts from the film, and so that they wouldn't have to pay royalties every time they screened the video, the band bought the rights to the film.

As a follow-up question, I would ask Mr. Mitzky whether law enforcement should have compensated the bands whose music they used during the siege of the church. Finally, I would also want to know if the song choice mattered less than the repetition or the volume. The three themes I would want to address would be the importance of genre, repetition, and volume.

After conducting a few interviews spread over a few months, confirmation with others on either side of the siege, and any follow-up questions, I would move on to the next stage of transcribing the data. Once the interviews had been analyzed, I would write a creative non-fiction piece about the experience, with the hope of transferability in developing a treatment for clients who have experienced trauma similar to Mr. Mitzky. For the sake of clarity, we can refer to this as "Involuntary Trauma". Of course, there are potential drawbacks to this study. Aside from the previously mentioned subject bias, I am susceptible to experimenter bias of which I will need to be aware. Similarly, Narrative Inquiry doesn't provide empirically based evidence, and many call into question the validity of the findings. Ultimately though, the information provided by Mr. Mitzky about his lived experience will be helpful in understanding and empathizing with someone who experienced involuntary or unorthodox forms of trauma.

Very few of our clients will be part of a siege from law enforcement. However, some clients will, unfortunately, be the recipients of psychological trauma, and music may very well have played a substantial role. Speaking with Mr. Mitzky about his experience, analyzing the themes, and writing about the data, will be able to provide a better understanding of the lived experience, so counselors may be more empathetic and develop suitable treatment plans.

References

Berggren. (2021). Musick Has Charms. *Voices (New York Folklore Society)*, 47(1-2), 18–18.

Buckley, K. (1992). *Panama: The Whole Story*. Simon & Schuster.

Cloonan, M., & Johnson, B. (2002). "Killing me softly with his song: An initial investigation into the use of popular music as a tool of oppression". *Popular Music, 21*(1), 27. Retrieved from https://tcsedsystem.id-m.oclc.org/login?
url=https://www.proquest.com/scholarly-jour-nals/killing-me-softly-with-his-song-initial/docview/195170131/se-2

Goodman, S. (2010). *Sonic warfare: Sound, affect, and the ecology of fear*. Cambridge, MA: MIT Press. Retrieved from https://tcsedsystem.idm.oclc.org/lo-gin?url=https://www.proquest.com/books/sonic-warfare-sound-affect-ecology-fear/docview/754032877/se-2

Haslbeck, Schmidli, L., Bucher, H. U., & Bassler, D. (2021). *Music Is Life—Follow-Up Qualitative Study on Parental Experiences of Creative Music Therapy in the Neonatal Period*. International Journal of Environmental Research and Public Health, 18(12), 6678–. https://doi.org/10.3390/ijerph18126678

Lale, & Ntourntoufis, P. (2020). "Individual music psychotherapy and psychosis: Understanding and measuring relative effectiveness through rates of readmission". *British Journal of Music Therapy (London, England: 1995)*, 34(1), 19–29. https://doi.org/10.1177/1359457520911011

LiKamWa, Cardoso, J., Sonke, J., Fillingim, R. B., & Booker, S. Q. (2022). The effect of music on pain sensitivity in healthy adults. *Arts & Health*, 14(1), 66–84. https://doi.org/10.1080/17533015.2020.1827278

Pelić, B. (2022). "Is Music the Barometer of Society? Exploring How Music Mirrored Society from the Ancient World, China to Central Europe in the 21st Century". *Comparative Civilizations Review*, (86), 6-22. Retrieved from: https://tcsedsystem.idm.oclc.org/login?url=https://www.proquest.com/scholarly-journals/is-music-barometer-society-exploring-how-mirrored/docview/2655181096/se-2

Qualitative study design: Narrative inquiry. LibGuides. (n.d.). Retrieved December 2, 2022, from *https://deakin.libguides.com/qualitative-study-designs/narrative-inquiry*

Schmid, Rosland, J. H., von Hofacker, S., Hunskår, I., & Bruvik, F. (2018). Patient's and health care provider's perspectives on music therapy in palliative care - an integrative review. *BMC Palliative Care*, 17(1), 32–32. https://doi.org/10.1186/s12904-018-0286-4

Sheperis, C., Young, J. S., & Daniels, M. H. (2017). *Counseling research: Quantitative, qualitative, and mixed methods*. Pearson.

Silverman. (2008). Quantitative Comparison of Cognitive Behavioral Therapy and Music Therapy Research: A Methodological Best-Practices Analysis to Guide Future Investigation for Adult Psychiatric Patients. *The Journal of Music Therapy*, 45(4), 457–506. https://doi.org/10.1093/jmt/45.4.457

Silverman. (2019). Quantitative comparison of group-based music therapy experiences in an acute care adult mental health setting: A four-group cluster-randomized study. *Nordic Journal of Music Therapy*, 28(1), 41–59. https://doi.org/10.1080/08098131.2018.1542614

Zuazu Bermejo, M. E. (2019). *Ruin sound: Audio afterlives, reenactment, and remembrance in the 210RW1S34RfeSDcfkexdo9rT3st 1RW1S34RfeSDcfkexdo9rT3Century* (Order No. 22620148). Available from ProQuest One Academic. (2316054722). Retrieved from https://tcsedsystem. idm.oclc.org/login?url=https://www.proquest.com/ dissertations-theses/ruin-sound-audio-afterlives-reen- actment/docview/2316054722/se-2

MORE RELEVANT MOVIE QUOTATIONS

These are quotations I tend to think about more now after I've been through a period of adjustment.

"Do you realize how much time we waste thinking about girls?"

Josh Hartnett's character, Matt, says this in the film *40 Days and 40 Nights* after he decides to give up all sexual activities for Lent. He makes this declaration while painting a model car he's just assembled and marveling about the amount of free time he has. Since my sex drive is non-existent, and it's still difficult to make emotional connections, I have removed "romantic relationship" from the list of priorities.

When people comment on how prolific I've been in terms of writing, etc., I often mention how there's a lot of time in a day when you don't have a spouse, children, or pets. It's still taking time to get used to this adjustment. So much of our conditioning throughout our lives focuses on finding a partner or starting a family. However, I've become much more comfortable with the idea it's not mandatory.

"They can't all be winners."

In the film *Bad Santa,* Billy Bob Thorton's character Willie says this to Therman Merman. The night before, Willie destroys Therman's advent calendar while drunk, and the following morning, he fixes it. Before he says that line, Therman opens that particular day's window to reveal a tic-tac. Willie says the line in reference to Therman's reaction to the tic-tac.

I think about this line sometimes when things don't play out as I've hoped. As the script for *Bad Santa* was being written, I don't know if the authors strove to include Buddhist tenets, but recognizing the reality of the world is one of the central ideals.

"You can't quit now. If for no other reason than to see a five megawatt laser fire just once."

In the film, *Real Genius,* students at a university based on Caltech, are tricked by their professor into designing a weapon for the government. When one of them is going to be flunked by the professor and suggests he'll probably just leave, the student's protégé suggests he can't leave, at least without seeing the project on which they've been working come to fruition. Of course, this all happens before the students discover they've been deceived.

This is one of the more profound quotations I think of frequently, since often it's difficult to find lasting motivation. One of the aspects of Somatic Experience Therapy that has been helpful is to remain curious about the unknown. So, I sometimes motivate myself by just thinking of the above line.

"I like simple pleasures."
Floyd Gondoli says this during a memorable scene in the film *Boogie Nights*. He's having a conversation with pornographic filmmaker, Jack Horner, trying to convince Jack they should do business together. Floyd says he doesn't want to reinvent the wheel or win an Academy Award. Among the simple pleasures he enjoys it's, "Butter in my ass and lollipops in my mouth."

As a species, we often think life is going to be full of revelatory grand moments; while there will be some, most of it will center on getting satisfaction from the simple pleasures. The phrase simple pleasures also reminds me of a story my cousin once told me. When my cousin lived on South Beach, his next-door neighbor was a model who was friends with singer David Lee Roth. Roth kept a kayak at the model's house and when he was on South Beach, would spend time kayaking in the ocean. One afternoon, my cousin was on the beach and spotted Roth sitting in his kayak while it was still tethered to the dock. They had previously been introduced, and my cousin called out asking how Roth was. The singer held up a lit joint and said, "Simple pleasures."

"You have an opportunity. This is a rebirth."

In the film, *Up in the Air,* George Clooney plays a character who helps companies have a smooth transition after firing an employee. In this particular scene, Clooney's suggests that a recently fired employee, rather than live a life of quiet desperation like Thoreau suggests, has the opportunity to follow his passion and do something that allows him to feel fulfilled. While it won't necessarily be easy, it will certainly be worthwhile in the long run. It will require the employee to make certain adjustments and reframe his perspective. I often consider this line when I need to find motivation.

"There are days when I do 24-hour stretches doing nothing but watching games on top of my regular job of accounting, which I do 60-70 hours a week."
Robert Mruczek says this about his weekly routine in the film _The King of Kong_. As one of the chief referees for the arcade company Twin Galaxies, he spends the majority of his time watching and verifying video game world records. He doesn't get paid, but it's a passion.

One of the things that had been on my mind these days is how to manage a work/life balance, which of course, reminds me of this quotation.

IMPROVED MORRIS

One of my favorite bands is named Sleep. They released an album in 1992 titled *Holy Mountain* that's considered a landmark record in the stoner metal category. After the release of *Holy Mountain*, they signed with a major label, London Records. Their follow-up album to *Holy Mountain*, called *Dopesmoker*, ended up being a single hour-long track. As they rehearsed and recorded it, the band needed to have the music charted out and they would name the sections. Morris, the section, was named after former Iron Man guitarist Alfred Morris. Along the way, as the section developed, they renamed it Improved Morris. The album's initial reception was complicated. However, in the twenty years since its release, *Dopesmoker* is considered a pinnacle of the genre. I look at the next section of my life as Improved Morris.

It is now February 2023. In June, it'll be five years since the aneurysm. So much has changed and while I will still get rattled, I have pretty much adjusted to everything. More importantly, I have coping strategies or people on whom I know will provide me support. One thing I think of frequently which helps both during stressful and enjoyable times is the Fourth Remembrance from a Buddhist teaching called The Five Remembrances. The first three are reminders that we will get sick, old, and eventually die. They address the physical nature of the world and our bodies. The Fourth Remembrance says, " All that is dear to me and everyone I love are of the nature to change. There is no way to escape being separated from them." I enjoy this interpretation, which I read from the Plum Village Website. Often, we fall prey to the idea that a bad experience will never end, or we hope to be able to hold onto or recapture elements of an enjoyable time. The Fourth Remembrance is a reminder that everything is transitory.

There had been a time when I couldn't imagine I would have a fulfilling future since it wasn't aligning with my expectations of what a fulfilling life would resemble. I recall enjoyable times with friends and family and hope I can recreate them. It isn't possible. That isn't to say I won't be able to have a similarly enjoyable time in the future. The uncertainty was difficult to accept, but ultimately that's part of what my Somatic Experience therapy has helped me to embrace.

Some aspects of my life are now completely different, but enough time has gone by that I don't notice them being strange. For example, my balance and vision are still compromised, but I have incorporated it into my everyday life. Instead of running for exercise, I use a stationary bike. The emotional disconnect is still present, but I have been able to recognize the emotions are still there; they are just more subtle and present themselves differently. Similarly, there has been a silver lining at times. Rather than become emotionally overwhelmed, I'm able to remain logical and stoic. A year ago, my mother was diagnosed with ALS. At one point, my brother, sister-in-law, and mother were thinking about the future and each was getting emotional. I handed out Kleenex similar to Elaine in the earlier scene, although I didn't wipe my mouth with it.

Since I turned forty, I had a ruptured brain aneurysm, there was a worldwide pandemic, my mother has been diagnosed with ALS, and just before his 80th birthday, my father broke his pelvis and shoulder. I had just begun a visit with my parents over Christmas vacation from school. I would have about three weeks with them. My father's injuries happened on the fourth day I was there. Instead of being able to decompress from exams and enjoy time with my parents, I became my mother's primary caretaker. My father returned a few weeks later in a wheelchair and both needed a full-time aide.

While some might think of the Taoist parable of the farmer I had mentioned in "Playing with House Money", this time I'll reference a saying I used to tell my high school students: "You can wish in one hand, and take a crap in the other, and see which gets filled first." It doesn't have the same poetry as the parable, but the message is just as clear. If aliens make first contact with us next year, I probably wouldn't bat an eyelash. It's been a rollercoaster ride, but I'm still curious as to what's next.

In a previous essay, I referenced the movie *Source Code* and how at times everything had so drastically changed within the last few years; sometimes it feels like I awoke on the wrong timeline. This is an essay I wrote about the same idea.

VAL KILMER'S ELBOW: THE DIALECTICS PART II

Recently, I'd been thinking of my former supervisor when I taught middle and high school, who was one of the nicest and most supportive people I'd ever met. She would sign every email or message with "Thank you for everything you do". Her exact opposite, somewhere in the multiverse, is a sociopathic investment banker who signs all his messages with "Thank you for nothing", followed by insults and profane statements. As I contemplated other differences within the multiverse, as well as causality and the lattice of coincidence, I thought of the original screenplay for *Rambo: First Blood, Part 2* before it had been extensively rewritten (the final script is credited to Kevin Jarre, James Cameron, and Sylvester Stallone).

(Spoiler alert!) In the novel *First Blood*, Rambo is killed by Sheriff Teasle. Similarly, in the original ending of the film *First Blood*, Rambo was supposed to die. The producers of the film *First Blood* had been able to cast Kirk Douglas as Colonel Trautman and had presold the foreign rights to the film based on Douglas's participation. When Stallone was cast as Rambo, Stallone argued for a new ending in which Rambo lived so there could be sequels. Kirk Douglas quit the film when producers changed the ending to have Rambo survive. Once Douglas quit, the producers were worried the film would collapse. (At the time, Kirk Douglas was a big name; Stallone had made a few films by then, including the first two *Rocky* movies, as well as *Paradise Alley,* but he wasn't yet a bankable action hero).

Later, when talks began about writing a sequel to *First Blood*, David Giler, a writer/producer, who had done uncredited rewrites on *First Blood*, recommended James Cameron write the screenplay for *First Blood: Part 2*. Cameron's draft had Rambo teamed up with a "techy" sidekick who producers thought might be portrayed by John Travolta since Travolta had previously worked with Stallone on *Staying Alive,* the sequel to *Saturday Night Fever*.

However, Stallone had had problems with Cameron's script, including the lack of political motives and "not much action" in the first third of the script. While Cameron eventually received a writing credit, who knows how much of his draft remained in the final product? Kevin Jarre would also get a story by credit, which probably meant he'd written a screenplay for a separate film in which elements had been incorporated into *First Blood: Part 2*.

Initially, in *First Blood: Part 2*, the character of Murdock was offered to Lee Marvin, who had also been considered for the role of Colonel Troutman in the original *First Blood*. Marvin would pass on the role, and Murdock would be portrayed by Charles Napier. Lee Marvin had also passed on the role of Quint in the film *Jaws*—Lee Marvin had been a sport fisherman and had scruples about Quint's demise in the film. Marvin had reportedly said, "The shark don't kill me; I kill the f—king shark." Whether he actually said this or not remains to be seen, but I like to imagine he did. Since he had been a Marine, Lee Marvin is buried in Arlington National Cemetery next to former Heavyweight Champion Joe Louis, who himself had been in the Army.

After *First Blood: Part 2*, many of the major players would work with each other on seminal projects. This is where causality, the collective unconscious, and the lattice of coincidence comes into play.

Before the filming of *First Bood: Part 2*, Stallone had been considered for *Beverly Hills Cop*. When he left that project, he used some of his ideas to make the film *Cobra*, which would be directed by George P. Cosmatos, the same director who had directed *First Blood: Part 2*. James Cameron would develop the story and direct another sequel for the *Alien* franchise *Aliens,* which was produced by David Giler. Kevin Jarre would write the screenplay and begin directing the film *Tombstone,* which co-starred Val Kilmer.

Val Kilmer's elbow is deformed as a result of Olecranon Bursitis after he'd broken his arm during the filming of *The Doors.* Jarre would be replaced as the director of *Tombstone* by George P. Cosmatos. I knew all this information off the top of my head; of course, it's only truly impressive if I perform its recitation in front of you like a magician performing sleight of hand.

Somewhere, in another dimension of the multiverse, my sociopathic supervisor is excoriating me for mishandling The Fisher Account. Later that night, I'll go home and watch a DVD I own of *First Blood: Part 2,* a cerebral film in which John Rambo, now joined by a techy sidekick, takes photos of a deserted POW camp in North Vietnam.

When I was in high school, there were only 49 graduating seniors, so each was allowed to have individual pages in the yearbook. I included two film quotations. The first was from *Enter the Dragon* in which actor Jim Kelly says, "I don't waste my time with it. When it comes, I won't even notice. I'll be too busy looking good." He's talking about how he never thinks about losing a fight. This doesn't really have an application to my life now, but it's definitely a great line.

I also included a quotation from *Fear and Loathing in Las Vegas*. "Every now and then when your life gets complicated and the weasels start closing in, the only cure is to load up on heinous chemicals and then drive like a bastard from Hollywood to Las Vegas ... with the music at top volume and at least a pint of ether."

At the age of eighteen, that seemed so romantic: writing, drinking, taking drugs, flaunting the law, and coming out virtually unscathed in the end. Now, I think of my life as a children's book in which the lead character discovers the magic has been with them all along. I don't need anything more to be fulfilled; I just need to continue to develop and be grateful for the things I already have. I also think of this Haiku by Mizuta Masahide. "Since my house burned down, I now own a better view of the rising moon."

Comedian Louis CK once mentioned during an interview about how there are three ways to deal with a traumatic experience: you can be crushed under it, you can be corroded by it, or you can get insight and develop self-reliance.

Though I've gained insight through some empirically supported methods, and developed self-reliance along the way, doesn't mean I've completely left mysticism behind. I'm still fascinated with the concept of synchronicity and other phenomenon. Sometimes, I also consider some of the goals I no longer pursue.

Years ago, I read an article by Chuck Klosterman in which he suggests the album *Kid A* by the band Radiohead accurately predicted the events of 9/11. It was a fascinating article that inspired me to write an essay about how the album *Third Eye Blind* by the band Third Eye Blind predicted the major events of my life. Each title corresponded to a major event.

Track 11: I Want You

After realizing I'd be truly happy just being on my own, I took myself out of circulation from the online dating world. Later, after the ruptured brain aneurysm, I returned to the dating world but again, that's another story. Regardless, nothing came from that endeavor either. Of course, this is all counterintuitive to the title of the song since it sounds like the narrator has found the person they would like to be in a relationship with. However, for me, I realized I needed to spend my time on other pursuits to make them worthwhile.

I would only focus on writing. It's like Rodney Dangerfield says in the film *Back to School*: "Always look out for number one, and be careful not to step in number two." I realized that the most important things to me were things I didn't share with anyone. Again, reflecting on this now, especially after the aneurysm and spending time with people who have significant others, I realize I'm an idiot.

Track 12: The Background

I reassessed my life in terms of the goals that are important to me and how I should spend my energy to achieve them. At the age of forty, it's nothing like how I imagined it would be when I was younger. I'm hoping my career will be similar to Robert Prosky's, a character actor whose first film role was the antagonist in the movie *Thief*. He got the role at the age of fifty-one.

There is a myriad of other people who didn't find any success in their fields until they were approaching middle age. I'm hoping this is closer to what will play out for me than, for example, Henry Darger, a custodian who died alone. Among his possessions was an unpublished manuscript of 15,145 pages separated into 15 volumes.

Track 13: Motorcycle Drive-By

I was on my way to visit my parents when I suffered from a ruptured brain aneurysm. I almost died. The only symptoms I had were very sudden; I began to sweat profusely, and I felt weak. Either way, I fell walking on the jetway to get on a plane. It's a good thing I didn't board. That was over two years ago, and it's still a surreal experience. I still haven't recovered fully either physically, or emotionally, and I may never will. Like a motorcycle drive-by, it happened quickly and changed my life. Or, perhaps, this song title represents the pandemic which was slower but just as much a life-altering predicament. There's also the distinct possibility this part of my life hasn't happened yet, and I'll be gunned down like the mobsters in the film *New Jack City*, who are shot to death in an actual motorcycle drive-by shooting.

Track 14: God of Wine

Over the last two and a half years, I have been reading a ton of philosophy to make sense of everything. From Aristotle and Nichomachean Ethics to Camus and the concept of the absurd. Nietzsche has some interesting thoughts, and he theorizes about The Apollonian and The Dionysian in his work *The Birth of Tragedy*. Dionysus is, among other things, the God of wine. This is probably the most literal of the song titles when alluding to the events of my life; the jury is still out on Motorcycle Drive-By.

In 1995, drummer Bill Berry, then with the band R.E.M., suffered a ruptured brain aneurysm while performing at a concert in Switzerland. Fortunately, he survived and recovered enough to rejoin the band.

However, he quit two years later, stating he didn't have the drive or desire that he once had to tour. I could definitely commiserate with Mr. Berry.

However, in 2022, Berry began to play music commercially with a new band The Bad Ends. Their debut album *The Power and The Glory* was released in 2023. Rather than interpret the song titles, I analyzed the lyrics using a modified version of the divination process with the *I Ching* or *The Book of Changes*. I had learned of that text while studying the concept of synchronicity: "the simultaneous occurrence of events which appear significantly related but have no discernable causal connection."

When divining, the reader uses a hexagram to determine which passage from the text to consult. Many commentators have used the book symbolically, often to provide guidance for moral decision-making as informed by Confucianism, Taoism, and Buddhism. Rather than use a hexagram, I analyzed the lyrics for any lines that resonated with me.

- "Mile Market 29" - *You could not begin again what couldn't be undone.*
- "All Your Friends are Dying" - *It wasn't anything I expected to hear.*
- "Left to be Found" - *Everyone you know says things behind your back, it's true.*

- "Thanksgiving 1915" - *And this goes to all those wishing there was a table set for them.*
- "The Ballad of Satan's Bride" - *Have you left the door to Satan open?*
- Ode to Jose - Instrumental
- "Little Black Cloud" - *It's been so long since you left no doubt, I bet your little black cloud's been lonesome.*
- "Honestly" - *I could have lent them out, but those are the sounds I can't live without. Too tempted to endure, but mostly I'm thrilled honestly.*
- "New York Murder Suicide" - *How can I get back to the place where once we so naive.*

I'm not going to provide any connotations or suggest any meaning behind any of the lyrics. When I was in graduate school for creative writing, I had a professor who would suggest edits by using an analogy of a Geiger counter. She would just say that a particular sentence or scene set off her Geiger counter and we should focus on further developing that sentence or scene. So, I'm going to take a page out of her book and just say the previous lyrics set off *my* Geiger counter.

I currently help run a website called Brain Stim. Every Monday, either I or the other administrator post three abstract thinking questions for people re-covering from brain injuries. One of the questions I posed a while back was: "If you had the opportunity to time travel, when/where would you go and what would you do? To make it easy, I said the space-time continuum wouldn't be affected, nor would you have to worry about the grandfather paradox or any other thought experiments which might hinder the best time available traveling through the cosmos.

I don't remember the various answers, though I'm sure they were profound. Without hesitating, I wrote I would have returned to the summer of 2000, after I had graduated from college and moved back in with my parents. Sometime between June, when I had fully settled in, and September, when I got a job working as a recruiter for software programmers. The following is a combination of two essays I wrote about the experience.

Some context might be important here before we get started. During my senior year of college, I had written, designed, and directed a one-act play titled *Show Me Your Tong Po*, which had had a week-long run in the school's black box theater. Additionally, I had won an award for outstanding creative writing for penning said play. So, after graduation, upon my return to New York City, it made complete sense to me that I would easily get a writing job, be it for tele-vision, film, or the stage.

In June, I moved back into my old bedroom in my

parent's apartment where I decided to be like the grasshopper from the fable *The Ant and The Grasshopper*. In the words of Tony Wilson from *24 Hour Party People*, "I don't want to say too much; I don't want to spoil it. I'll just say one word: 'Icarus'. If you get it, great. If you don't, that's fine too. But you should probably read more."

An average weekday would begin at the gym: three days on and one day off. Day 1 consisted of chest and triceps, Day 2 was back and biceps, and Day 3 was core and legs. Cardiovascular was shunned outright. Next up was the Nintendo 64. While I had been at school, a new software named "Napster" had been created. Using the software would allow anyone to download and play any song ever recorded for free. It took a little while to select an adequate playlist, but over a few days, the following gems were compiled: "Abracadabra" by The Steve Miller Band, "I'm Blue" by Eiffel 65, "Funk That" by Sagat, and a freestyle rap by Eminem.

At one point, Dante and my brother and I recorded our own music as a rap group named The Artificial Implants. I was "DJ Scratch and Sniff" and Dante was "MC Clean-X". My brother was named "Poochie". One day, Dante asked for my brother to "kick it for us hard". My brother misheard what Dante had said, a mondegreen, and it became the title of our song "Kick This Horse Hard." From what I remember, the lyrics were "Went to the stable last night / did not put up a fight / I just went to the horse / and I kicked 'em." The chorus was "Kick this horse hard / kick 'em, kick 'em, kick 'em" times two.

At the time the game had been released, The New York Yankees had become one of the most dominant franchises of the century. From 1996 to 2001, they would win the World Series four out of five times, including three in a row. In fact, in their first four appearances, they won 16 out of 17 games. They lost a single game to the New York Mets in the 2000 series. This definitely factored in my friend's and my decision to choose them. Dante and I had also decided to play as teammates instead of playing as opponents. We would take turns pitching, and we would alternate. Similarly, we had split up the batters: Dante had all of the odd batters and I would take the even. As the Nintendo Baseball season progressed, I had the sense this was shaping up to be possibly the greatest summer of my life. It was a privilege of youth, right after college graduation but right before obligations becomes one of the primary life motivators.

As the New York Yankees, Dante and I pretty much dominated every other team. We had to have lost some games, though I don't remember us losing. Sports records that had existed untouched for years were shattered; no record stood a chance. For example, at the time, the single-season home run record had been 70. It had been set by Mark McGuire in

1998. He and Sammy Sosa had gone back and forth in a tight race before McGuire finally took the lead. Before that, Roger Maris's record of 61—which had been set in 1961—had stood for 37 years.

Barry Bonds would eventually break McGuire's record by hitting 73 home runs in 2001. Of course, the records set by Sosa, McGuire, and Bonds were tainted during accusations and a Congressional investigation that stipulated they had all taken performance-enhancing drugs. In Dante's and my game, designated hitter Chili Davis had already hit close to fifty home runs, and we hadn't even arrived at the All-Star Break. It was going to be a great summer full of promise. Then, the unthinkable happened. The game had a glitch, and we couldn't save our season. We still had over half the season to go. Aside from the death of loved ones and other tragedies, it may have been the most catastrophic thing to happen in my life up until that point.

The funny/sad thing is you probably think I'm kidding. We tried and failed in all our repeated attempts to continue playing the game. Dante, my younger brother, and I tried all of the methods we knew—blowing on the cartridge, hitting reset, unplugging the game. There were probably some other unorthodox techniques straight out of an episode of *MacGyver*, but I think I've blocked most of the unpleasantness from my memory.

A few weeks later, Dante got a job working in finance, and our summer plans changed. He could no longer join me for Nintendo 64. By the end of the month, I too would enter the workforce, and I would have to "put childish things away". While it may seem hyperbolic, playing All-Star Baseball '99 was like The Woodstock Rock Festival. For us, All-Star Baseball '99 symbolized a time with no ulterior motives or compromises; chock full of pure idealism. The glitch in the game was like the Altamont Free Concert which ended in tragedy, and many historians point to it as a symbol for the end of the Woodstock era. Sometimes, I reflect on this time as a way to keep perspective about the important things, and what that time in my life represented. I also think of the closing words of Henry David Thoreau in his essay *Walking*. "So we saunter toward the Holy Land, till one day the sun shall shine more brightly than ever he has done, shall perchance shine into our minds and hearts, and light up our whole lives with a great awakening light, as warm and serene and golden as on a bankside in autumn." Who knows? Maybe there will be a game console there too.

It goes without saying some days are still difficult. Just today, for the first time in a long time, I felt truly overwhelmed. However, I was able to eventually get my bearings. There are no finish lines to cross. To quote Robin Williams character Mr. Keating in the film *Dead Poet's Society*: "That the powerful play goes on, and you get to contribute a verse". It's good to have strategies to employ when the proverbial weasels start closing in, though, they don't necessarily need to include hallucinogens or ether. It's difficult to keep things in perspective while you're still going through them, but if there are two suggestions I can give you it's to remember that things will change, and to focus on the simple pleasures. The following is another essay I wrote about doing just that.

THERE ARE 106 MILES TO CHICAGO

We have a full tank of gas, half a pack of cigarettes, it's dark, and we're wearing sunglasses. The previous sentence, including the title of this piece, is spoken by Elwood Blues in the film *The Blues Brothers* as they are about to race to the Cook County property assessor's office to save the Catholic orphanage in which the brothers had been raised. By the way, in the movie, the clerk at the assessor's office is played by Steven Spielberg.

I thought of this line recently while my mother and I were on a road trip to visit my brother and his family. One of the more enjoyable moments of many I share with my mother is when I play music for her. She has been gracious enough to be a guest on my podcast, A Fistful of Faceful but, more often than not, we listen to music while driving. She's a huge fan of Billy Joel, but that doesn't stop me from going directly to Ozzy's Boneyard on the radio. Although, these days, we tend to listen to The Bridge. Often, I'll inundate her with trivia about songs; for example, if we listen to a Fleetwood Mac song, I'll remind her the band name came from Peter Green, one of the original guitarists, who named the group after his two friends, and bandmates, Mick Fleetwood and John McVie. Or when "Alone Again Naturally" came on, I told her Gilbert O'Sullivan sued Biz Markie for sampling the music for Markie's song "Alone Again". The verdict, which ruled in O'Sullivan's favor, became a landmark Supreme Court decision in which all samples needed to be cleared. Up until that point, music could be sampled without compensating the original artist. On other occasions, our sessions can resemble an Abbott and Costello routine. When giving her a clue to guess the band KISS, I said:

> Andrew: "Think painted faces."
> Mom: "I've never heard of them."
> Andrew: "Green Light".
> Mom: "I haven't heard of them either"
> Andew: "No, you have a green light."

More recently, we revisited Ozzy's Boneyard which produced this gem.

> Andrew: "Awesome! 'Walk' by Pantera."

Mom: "'Walk' by Pantera?"
Andrew: "No. 'Walk' is the song. The Band
is Pantera. The opening line is 'Can't you see
I'm easily bothered by persistence.'"
Mom: "Why didn't you give me time to guess
that?"

Another memorable moment from the trip occurred when we were at my brother's house. The three of us played the card game Milles Borne, which we used to play frequently when we were much younger. The object of the game is to win a race by accumulating a thousand miles. Along the way, your opponents can sabotage your trip by giving you hazard cards which include a flat tire, out of gas, a speed limit of 50 mph, and a stop light. My brother's favorite part of the game, this time around, was giving hazard cards to both me and my mother. A player can only suffer one hazard card at a time, but I said we should amend that rule. While someone's flat tire is being fixed, why not be able to puncture their other tires or siphon gas from their tank?

We ended up sticking with the original rules, but it reminded me of other enjoyable moments I had spent with my brother throughout the years. Many of us spend a lot of our time trying to replicate those moments. Sean Carswell once wrote an excellent short story entitled "The Fiction of Old Friends" about his friendship with my cousin Mark. In it he wrote, "I assumed Mark to be a static character. Like Sal Paradise in *On the Road*, Mark should be the exact same Mark every time I chose to pick that book up ... I realized that the characters who are our friends are constantly being rewritten, growing, developing further with a mass of back story that never makes it into the draft we get to read."

Dealing with this phenomenon was magnified while I recovered from a ruptured brain aneurysm, and I had difficulty adjusting. Over time, as my brain healed, I was able to wrap my mind around it. Certain things will never change; others will, but they can always be enjoyable. My brother and I may not play prison rules Milles Borne, I may or may not continue to inundate my mother with music trivia, but the opportunities for wonder will continue to exist.

We had Thanksgiving of 2022 at my brother's house. He and I had a poignant conversation of how it would probably be the last family Thanksgiving he would host since it would be extremely difficult for my mother to travel in the future. However, there will be other opportunities to experience joy, sadness, fulfillment, and more.

F. Scott Fitzgerald had been working on the novel *The Last Tycoon* before he died. The novel was published posthumously and in Fitzgerald's notes was the phrase, "There are no second acts in American lives." I'm almost certain the line has been misinterpreted, but the consensus has been to take the line at face value. I've been fortunate enough to have a second act, and I'm going to make the most of the opportunity using insight, self-reliance, and a sense of wonder. It certainly won't look like what I had imagined, but I'm curious to see where it goes.

ABOUT THE AUTHOR

Andrew Davie has worked in theater, finance, and education. He taught English in Macau on a Fulbright Grant, at the university level in New York and Hong Kong, and at the middle/high school level in Virginia. Currently, he's pursuing his Clinical Mental Health Counseling Degree, and has survived a ruptured brain aneurysm and subarachnoid hemorrhage.

He has published short stories in various places, a memoir and addendum, and crime fiction books with All Due Respect, Close to the Bone, Alien Buddha Press, and Next Chapter. He also co-hosts a music review show called Happy Hour with Heather and Guest.

To learn more about Andrew Davie and discover more Next Chapter authors, visit our website at www.nextchapter.pub.

The Second Act
ISBN: 978-4-82418-761-1
Large Print

Published by
Next Chapter
2-5-6 SANNO
SANNO BRIDGE
143-0023 Ota-Ku, Tokyo
+818035793528

29th September 2023